ANIMALS AND THEIR HABITATS
Tropical Regions and Rain Forests

WORLD
BOOK

A Scott Fetzer company
Chicago
www.worldbookonline.com

World Book, Inc.
233 N. Michigan Avenue
Chicago, IL 60601
U.S.A.

For information about other World Book publications,
visit our website at http://www.worldbookonline.com
or call 1-800-WORLDBK (967-5325).

For information about sales to schools and libraries, call
1-800-975-3250 (United States), or 1-800-837-5365 (Canada).

Staff

Executive Committee
President: Donald D. Keller
Vice President and Editor in Chief: Paul A. Kobasa
Vice President, Marketing/Digital Products: Sean Klunder
Vice President, International: Richard Flower
Controller: Yan Chen
Director, Human Resources: Bev Ecker

Editorial

Associate Director, Supplementary Publications:
  Scott Thomas
Managing Editor, Supplementary Publications:
  Barbara A. Mayes
Associate Manager, Supplementary Publications:
  Cassie Mayer
Editors: Brian Johnson and Kristina Vaicikonis
Researcher: Annie Brodsky
Editorial Assistant: Ethel Matthews
Manager, Contracts & Compliance
  (Rights & Permissions): Loranne K. Shields
Manager, Indexing: David Pofelski
Writer: David Alderton
Project Editor: Sarah Uttridge
Editorial Assistant: Kieron Connolly
Design: Andrew Easton

Graphics and Design

Senior Manager: Tom Evans
Senior Designer: Don Di Sante
Manager, Cartography: Wayne K. Pichler
Senior Cartographer: John Rejba

Pre-Press and Manufacturing

Director: Carma Fazio
Manufacturing Manager: Steven K. Hueppchen
Senior Production Manager: Janice Rossing
Production/Technology Manager: Anne Fritzinger
Proofreader: Emilie Schrage

Library of Congress Cataloging-in-Publication Data
Tropical regions and rain forests.
    p. cm. -- (Animals and their habitats)
    Summary: "This illustrated volume is an introduction to
the animal life of the tropics and particularly the tropical rain
forest. Detailed captions describe each animal, while inset
maps show where the animals can be found around the
world. Features include a glossary, maps, photographs, and
an index"--Provided by publisher.
    Includes index.
    ISBN 978-0-7166-0449-5
    1. Rain forest animals--Juvenile literature. 2. Rain forest
ecology--Juvenile literature. I. World Book, Inc.
QL112.T76 2012
591.734--dc23
                        2012005839

Animals and Their Habitats
Set ISBN: 978-0-7166-0441-9

Printed in China by Leo Paper Products LTD.,
Heshan, Guangdong
lst printing July 2012

Cover image: The mountain gorilla is
one of the most endangered animals of
the tropical rain forest. Rain forests are
being destroyed so quickly that many
species are becoming extinct before
scientists can even identify them.

© blickwinkel/Alamy

Contents

Introduction

Rain forests are the richest areas of life on our planet. More *species* (kinds) of amphibians, birds, insects, mammals, and reptiles live in rain forests than anywhere else. Rain forests cover only 6 to 7 percent of the world's surface but support more than half of the world's plant and animal species. Scientists believe millions more rain forest species remain undiscovered.

Rain forests grow in the tropics, a region that extends about 1,600 miles (2,570 kilometers) north and south of the equator. Tropical regions include Central America, much of South America, and most of Africa. The tropics also include Southeast Asia, northern Australia, and parts of India, as well as many islands.

The tropics are warm, with little change in temperature during the year. Many tropical areas receive huge amounts of rain, with thundershowers occuring more than 200 days a year. Such areas may receive more than 80 inches (203 centimeters) of rain each year. These conditions have enabled vast rain forests to grow.

Rain forests are made up of several levels, each of which provides a different *habitat* (living place). Abundant sunlight reaches the tallest trees, which can be up to 265 feet (80 meters) tall. By contrast, the lowest levels are surprisingly dark, with as little as 1 percent of the sunlight available higher up.

The creatures of the upper layers of the rain forest are much different from the creatures that live on the forest floor. Monkeys swing athletically from branch to branch. Fruit bats are quite common, as are thousands of species of birds, many of them exotic. The male Ragianna bird-of-paradise has long reddish plumes and tail feathers to attract a mate. But this bird must watch for birds of prey, which soar above the canopy. Snakes also move among the branches, ready to strike.

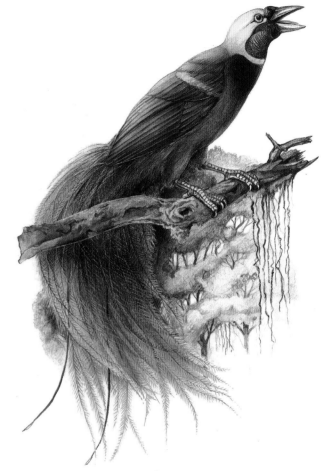

RAGGIANA BIRD-OF-PARADISE

PANGOLIN

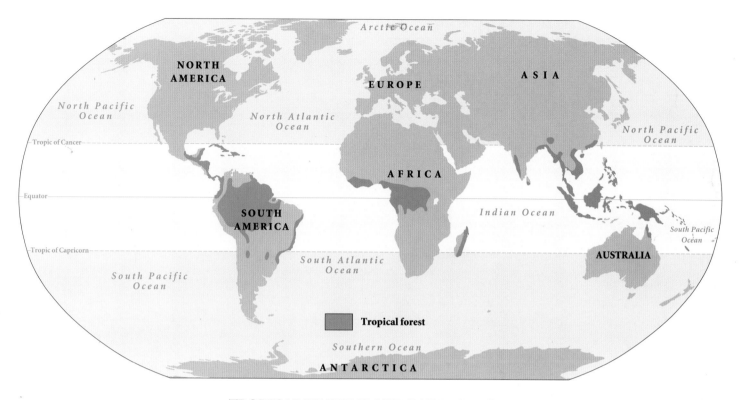

TROPICAL REGIONS AND RAIN FORESTS

RING-TAILED LEMUR

The lower levels of the rain forest support some of the largest animals on Earth. These include elephants and gorillas. Fearsome *predators* (hunting animals) hide in the gloom and leaf litter, ready to ambush prey. These include tigers, jaguars, and boa constrictors.

Animals of the rain forest have developed various *adaptations* (characteristics) to avoid being eaten. Poison dart frogs are brightly colored, to warn predators of the poison in their skin. Pangolins are covered in horny scales and can roll into an armored ball.

Tragically, people are rapidly destroying the world's rain forests. This loss of habitat threatens many animals and plants. In fact, scientists believe that many species are disappearing before they can be identified. Many people are working to save rain forests and the remarkable creatures that live in them.

Huon Tree Kangaroo

Some kangaroos live among the treetops, leaping from branch to branch. Kangaroos are *marsupials,* a type of mammal that gives birth to tiny young that finish growing in the mother's pouch.

VITAL STATISTICS

WEIGHT	15–22 lb (7–10 kg); females are larger
LENGTH	37–66 in (93–168 cm), including a tail almost as long as the body
SEXUAL MATURITY	2 years
LENGTH OF PREGNANCY	39–45 days; newborns measure 1 in (2.5 cm) long
NUMBER OF OFFSPRING	1
DIET	Eats mainly leaves; also feeds on fruits, nuts, insects, and bird eggs
LIFESPAN	Up to 14 years

ANIMAL FACTS

The Huon tree kangaroo is well *adapted* (suited) to life among the trees. It is graceful and can leap up to 30 feet (9 meters) between branches. It can jump to the ground from a height of 60 feet (18 meters) without injury. On the ground, these kangaroos walk rather than hop. They have a longer pregnancy than other marsupials, though the young are still tiny at birth. The young, called *joeys,* remain in the pouch for nearly a year. These kangaroos have become *endangered* (at risk of dying out) because of hunting and the loss of their forest homes.

Strong claws help the kangaroo climb, but the foot lacks thumbs for grasping branches.

WHERE IN THE WORLD?

Found only in Papua New Guinea, on the Huon Peninsula and the nearby island of Umboi.

NOSE
The nose is large and pink, with large nostrils.

COLORATION
The back is chestnut to red-brown, with a yellowish tail, belly, and feet.

LIMB LENGTH
Unlike other kangaroos, tree kangaroos have forelimbs almost as long as their hind limbs.

BACK
Fur grows in opposite directions on this part of the body, allowing rainwater to run off the coat efficiently.

TAIL
The tail is long and tube-like. It is used for balance rather than grasping tree branches.

HOW BIG IS IT?

CLIMBING
Tree kangaroos use both their front and hind legs to move around among the trees.

Gaur

SPECIES • *Bos gaurus*

VITAL STATISTICS

WEIGHT	1,540–2,200 lb (700–1,000 kg); cows are generally lighter
LENGTH	8–11 ft (2.5–3.3 m), including tail
SEXUAL MATURITY	2–3 years
LENGTH OF PREGNANCY	About 275 days; weaning occurs 7–9 months later
NUMBER OF OFFSPRING	Usually 1 calf, occasionally 2
DIET	Eats grass and other plant matter
LIFESPAN	Potentially up to 30 years

This wild ox of Asia is a shy giant, with males reaching up to 2,200 pounds (1,000 kilograms). It has been *domesticated* (tamed) in India and serves as a beast of burden known as the "gayal."

WHERE IN THE WORLD?

Lives in southern Asia, from India across parts of Southeast Asia into Vietnam and Malaysia.

ANIMAL FACTS

Gaurs live in herds that usually have about 10 members, though large herds may have up to 40 gaurs. The herds are led by the largest male. Other adult males stay outside the herd, living on their own. The great size of adults makes them dangerous prey, though *predators* (hunting animals) do attack calves. The greatest danger to gaurs comes from human beings. People hunt the animals and destroy their forest *habitat* (living place). Fewer than 20,000 gaurs are thought to survive in the wild, and these animals live in isolated pockets.

HORNS
These are massive and curved, growing to a length of about 32 inches (80 centimeters). They grow from the side of the head rather than the top.

HEIGHT
The shoulder height can be more than 79 inches (200 centimeters). Those in southeastern Asia are largest.

SOCIAL STRUCTURE
Gaurs generally live in herds headed by a male.

HOW BIG IS IT?

HEAVYWEIGHTS
Although the sheer size of the ox deters most predators, tigers may attack an adult gaur. However, the tigers prefer to prey on smaller, weaker calves.

Both males and females have horns.

Malayan Tapir

VITAL STATISTICS

WEIGHT	550–660 lb (250–300 kg); males are bigger
LENGTH	6.2–8.2 ft (1.9–2.5 m); up to 42 in (105 cm) tall at the shoulder
SEXUAL MATURITY	2.5–3.5 years
LENGTH OF PREGNANCY	390–400 days; young are mainly brown
NUMBER OF OFFSPRING	1; weaning occurs at 6–8 months
DIET	Eats mainly grasses, aquatic plants, twigs, and leaves
LIFESPAN	Up to 30 years

ANIMAL FACTS

Although the tapir looks like a pig, it is more closely related to horses and rhinos. It can climb steep mountain tracks without difficulty. It tends to move higher onto such *terrain* (area of land) during the wet season. The tapir also swims well. It frequently *wallows* (rolls about) in water and feeds on *aquatic* (water) plants. Tapirs communicate with whistling sounds, and they mark their *territory* (personal area) with urine. If threatened, they can run quickly. They are vulnerable to tigers, which may stalk them on the forest floor. However, the largest threat to tapirs comes from people. Human beings have cut down the forests where they live, replacing them with palm oil plantations. Tapirs are also threatened by *poaching* (illegal hunting). The Malayan tapir is now *endangered* (at risk of dying out).

These creatures of the forest are usually found close to water. They are hard to observe, partly because they are shy and active at night. They also have become rare as much of the forest has been destroyed.

WHERE IN THE WORLD?

Southeast Asia, from Myanmar (also known as Burma) down into parts of Sumatra, in Indonesia.

NOSE
The tapir uses its long, sensitive nose to pick up food.

TAIL
The tail is short and curls around the rump.

HOOFS
Nails jut from the legs on either side of the hoofs.

COLORATION
The coat has a distinctive black and white pattern. This pattern helps to *camouflage* (disguise) the tapir at night.

HOW BIG IS IT?

MEETING UP

Tapirs are usually solitary, except for the breeding season. Males and females may circle and nip at each other's ears and flanks.

Babirusa

VITAL STATISTICS

WEIGHT	130–220 lb (60–100 kg)
LENGTH	35–40 in (87–100 cm), including tail; up to 32 in (80 cm) tall
SEXUAL MATURITY	5–10 months
LENGTH OF PREGNANCY	155–175 days; weaning occurs 6.5–8 months later
NUMBER OF OFFSPRING	Usually 1–2
DIET	Eats mainly fruit, grasses, roots, and fungi
LIFESPAN	10–14 years

The babirusa is a wild Asian hog. Its long *canine* (biting) teeth form jutting tusks. The upper canines actually pierce through the top of the snout and curve back over the face.

WHERE IN THE WORLD?

Lives in Indonesia, mainly on the islands of Sulawesi and Buru.

ANIMAL FACTS

The babirusa is a hog of the forest. It lives only on certain islands in Indonesia. Males are usually solitary, while females live in small family groups. The largest female leads the group. Babirusas build straw nests, where they sleep and shelter from the tropical rain. Babirusas run well, and they are strong swimmers. Pythons are among the *predators* (hunting animals) that prey on babirusas, especially the young. Babirusas have suffered from hunting and destruction of their forest *habitats* (living places). They are protected by law, but only a few thousand are thought to remain in the wild.

TUSKS
The razor-like upper tusks look more like antlers than teeth. The name *babirusa* means *pig-deer*.

TAIL
The tail is long and tapers significantly along its length.

SNOUT
Broad nostrils help detect scents. Unlike some other hogs, babirusas cannot dig well with their snouts.

HAIR
The amount of hair varies significantly between individuals. Some are nearly bald.

FIGHTING
The bottom canines are used for slashing attacks during fights between rival males. The upper canines help to protect the face.

These hogs rub their cheeks on the ground, which is thought to leave scent that marks their *territory* (personal area).

HOW BIG IS IT?

Asian Elephant

Asian elephants were *domesticated* (tamed) thousands of years ago. They have served as beasts of burden, weapons of war, and symbols of royalty. These magnificent animals are now endangered in the wild.

VITAL STATISTICS

Weight	6,600–8,000 lb (3,000–3600 kg)
Length	18–21 ft (5.5–6.5 m); stands up to 9.8 ft (3 m) tall at the shoulder
Sexual Maturity	Around 14 years
Length of Pregnancy	18–22 months
Number of Offspring	1; weaning occurs by 4 years
Diet	Eats up to 331 lb (150 kg) of grasses and leaves a day
Lifespan	About 65 years

ANIMAL FACTS

The Asian elephant's trunk is remarkably useful. It is used for eating, drinking, breathing, smelling, touching, calling, and washing. Asian elephants form herds of about 20 or more female relatives and their young. The herd is led by the oldest female, who directs the search for food and water. Asian elephants are *endangered* (at risk of dying out), with only about 50,000 elephants remaining in the wild. They are threatened by loss of their forest *habitats* (living places) and illegal hunting for their tusks.

Asian elephants (left) have just a single, upper "finger" on their trunk. African elephants (right) have two.

WHERE IN THE WORLD?

Once found from Iran through India to Southeast Asia and China; now exists in only isolated populations in India and Southeast Asia.

SKIN
Tough and grayish-brown, with a scattering of stiff, dark hair.

FEET
The feet are large and circular, with four toes on the hind feet. African elephants have only three toes on the hind feet.

EARS
The ears are smaller than those of African elephants.

TUSKS
Only the males grow large tusks. These unusual *incisors* (biting teeth) may reach 5 feet (1.5 meters) long. Not all males grow tusks.

DIVING DEEPER
Asian elephants can swim well. They use their trunk like a snorkel to breathe air as they swim.

HOW BIG IS IT?

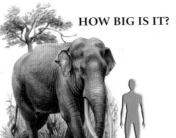

Bengal Tiger

The Bengal tiger is the most common *subspecies* (variety) of tiger, though it, like all other tigers, is *endangered* (at risk of dying out). The Bengal tiger is a national symbol of Bangladesh and India.

VITAL STATISTICS

WEIGHT	Females 220–400 lb (100–180 kg); males 368–485 lb (167–220 kg)
LENGTH	5–6 ft (1.5–1.8 m); tail is 2-3 ft (0.6–0.9 m); up to 4 ft (1.2 m) tall
SEXUAL MATURITY	3 years
LENGTH OF PREGNANCY	90–105 days
NUMBER OF OFFSPRING	Average 3–4, but can be up to 6; weaning at around 90 days
DIET	Prefers larger mammal prey
LIFESPAN	Usually 10–12 years

WHERE IN THE WORLD?

Found mainly in areas of India and Bangladesh.

ANIMAL FACTS

Although tigers are the largest cats in the world, these solitary beasts hunt by stealth at night. They approach prey silently, hiding behind cover until the last moment. Then they leap and bite their victim on the neck. They feed on deer, hogs, water buffalo, and a variety of other animals. In rare cases, they have attacked and eaten people. Tigers also swim and climb well. Fewer than 2,500 Bengal tigers are thought to remain in the wild. They are threatened mainly by *poaching* (illegal hunting) for their fur and body parts. They also are threatened by the loss of their forest *habitat* (living place).

A tiger tries to capture its prey by biting its neck.

COLORATION
The fur is a rich shade of orange-brown, with black stripes.

TAIL
The tail helps the tiger maintain its balance. It reaches about 3 feet (0.9 meter) long.

WHISKERS
These help the tiger to move through the forest by sense of touch, which is especially useful at night.

TEETH
Sharp *canine* (biting) teeth at the corners of the mouth make for a deadly bite.

HOW BIG IS IT?

BY HIS STRIPES

Zookeepers and wildlife officials can tell tigers apart by the animals' facial stripes. These stripes are unique to each individual, like a person's fingerprints.

Jaguar

VITAL STATISTICS

WEIGHT	90–300 lb (40–140 kg)
LENGTH	5–8.5 ft (1.6–2.6 m)
SEXUAL MATURITY	3–4 years
LENGTH OF PREGNANCY	93–105 days
NUMBER OF OFFSPRING	1–4
DIET	Feeds on a variety of mammals; also eats fish, turtles, and *crocodilians* (crocodile-like reptiles)
LIFESPAN	10–12 years in the wild

The jaguar is the largest, most powerful wild cat of the Western Hemisphere. The jaguar symbolized power and courage to the ancient Maya, who considered the animal sacred.

WHERE IN THE WORLD?

Lives in parts of Mexico extending into Central America, down across South America to the northern tip of Argentina.

ANIMAL FACTS

Jaguars usually hunt at dawn and dusk. They eat almost any kind of animal, including armadillos, deer, fish, wild pigs, tapirs, turtles, and capybaras and other rodents. Their markings make them difficult to spot in dense jungle, and they usually sneak up on prey or drop down on it from above. Some jaguars are entirely black. These cats are often called black panthers, but they belong to the same *species* (kind) as the spotted cats. Jaguars have fallen in numbers, and they are no longer found in many areas. Many jaguars are killed by ranchers, as the cats may feed on cattle.

COAT
The body is covered with "spots" called *rosettes.* The tail is banded with black markings and ends in a dark tip.

HIND LEGS
Powerful leg muscles enable these cats to climb, jump, and swim well.

MOUTH
Exceptionally strong jaws enable the jaguar to crack the shells of turtles and *tortoises* (land turtles).

HOW BIG IS IT?

HUNTING TECHNIQUE
Jaguars often hunt near water, leaping down on their prey from an overhanging branch. They are perfectly comfortable in the water.

Jaguars (left) look much like the leopards of Africa (right), but their heads are usually somewhat rounder.

Clouded Leopard

SPECIES • *Neofelis nebulosa*

The clouded leopard is rarely seen as it moves like a ghost through the forest. The cat is a strong and graceful climber that spends much of its time in the trees.

VITAL STATISTICS

WEIGHT	35–50 lb (16–23 kg)
LENGTH	4–6.5 ft (1.2–2.0 m), including tail
SEXUAL MATURITY	2–3 years
LENGTH OF PREGNANCY	86–93 days
NUMBER OF OFFSPRING	1–5
DIET	Hunts birds, deer, monkeys, porcupines, squirrels, and wild pigs
LIFESPAN	Probably 7–10 years; has lived up to 17 years in captivity

ANIMAL FACTS

Clouded leopards have strong legs, large paws, and tough claws. These provide them with a firm grip on tree bark, enabling them to climb down trees headfirst. They also can hang upside down on the underside of branches. Clouded leopards roar but they cannot purr. The cats are usually solitary, except during the breeding season. Young clouded leopards have more obvious patterning than adults. The young remain with their mother for about 10 months. Clouded leopards are *vulnerable* (at risk) to extinction. Their numbers are falling because the forests in which they live are being destroyed. They also are hunted and trapped illegally for their fur and body parts.

WHERE IN THE WORLD?

Lives in Southeast Asia, from Nepal and southern China, across the Malay Peninsula.

PATTERNING
The common name of these cats comes from their dark spots, which are said to resemble clouds.

LEGS AND PAWS
The legs are stocky, with broad paws. The tough pads protect the feet from injury.

TAIL
The clouded leopard's long tail helps the animal keep its balance when leaping from one branch to another.

HOW BIG IS IT?

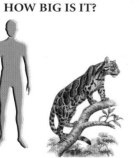

GROWING UP

Young clouded leopards do not open their eyes until 12 days after birth. They start taking solid food at 10 weeks old.

Bush Dog

SPECIES • *Speothos venaticus*

VITAL STATISTICS

WEIGHT	10–15 lb (5–7 kg); males are slightly larger
LENGTH	25–35 in (68–88 cm); may stand only 10 in (25 cm) tall
SEXUAL MATURITY	1 year
LENGTH OF PREGNANCY	63 days; weaning occurs at 8 weeks
NUMBER OF OFFSPRING	Up to 6
DIET	Hunts mainly rodents, such as pacas
LIFESPAN	Up to 10 years in captivity

Although bush dogs are rare, they are found across much of South America. These short-legged dogs of the forest live in *packs* (groups) of up to a dozen individuals.

WHERE IN THE WORLD?

Ranges over a wide area in southern Central America and South America, down to northeastern Argentina.

ANIMAL FACTS

Bush dogs are rarely seen by people because the animals are small and shy. They have many hiding places in the rain forest, including hollow logs and the abandoned *burrows* (underground shelters) of other animals. Bush dogs have a distinctive whining call, which they use to keep in touch with each other. Females raise pups in burrows or hollow logs. The males hunt and bring back food. The number of bush dogs is falling because of rain forest destruction and pollution.

Bush dogs mark their *territory* (personal area) by backing up to a tree, standing on their front legs, and urinating on it.

FACE
Bush dogs have broad nostrils, which help them pick up the trails of prey on the forest floor. They also have powerful, compact jaws.

EARS
The ears are relatively small, set low and located well back on the skull.

COLORATION
Adults are tan in color, but pups are dark gray at birth.

HINDQUARTERS
These are well-muscled, helping the bush dog run or swim efficiently.

HOW BIG IS IT?

WATER SPORTS
The toes of bush dogs are webbed, which adds to their swimming ability. They do not hesitate to pursue capybaras and other prey into the water.

Common Vampire Bat

SPECIES • *Desmodus rotundus*

Despite its frightening reputation, the vampire bat is not a threat to people or animals. This tiny, fragile mammal feeds on only small amounts of blood at a time. However, its bite can spread disease.

VITAL STATISTICS

WEIGHT	Typically 2 oz (57 g) but can double after feeding
LENGTH	3.5 in (9 cm); wingspan of 7 in (18 cm)
SEXUAL MATURITY	9–10 months
LENGTH OF PREGNANCY	About 217 days; mothers fly with their newborn offspring, clasping them
NUMBER OF OFFSPRING	1–2; weaning occurs at 1 month
DIET	Blood
LIFESPAN	Up to 12 years

WHERE IN THE WORLD?

Ranges from Mexico south across Central America into South America, to Chile and Argentina.

ANIMAL FACTS

The vampire bat is unusual in that it feeds entirely on blood. It is quiet and graceful. The bat usually lands on the ground near sleeping cattle and horses. It then climbs up the body of the sleeping animal, taking care not to disturb its victim. The bat pierces the skin with its razor-sharp teeth. The bite rarely wakes the animal. The bat is then able to lap up the blood with its tongue. A special substance in the saliva helps to keep the blood flowing. Blood is not very nourishing, so the bat must feed frequently. It can drink half its body weight in blood in only 20 minutes.

Hook-like claws help the bat to haul itself up onto prey.

WINGS
A bat's wings are highly modified arms and hands. Long arm and finger bones support the wings, giving them their shape. A thin membrane of skin connects these bones to one another and the bat's body, forming the wing's surface.

NOSE
The nose has a heat sensor that allows the bat to locate blood beneath the skin of other animals.

TONGUE
The bat uses its tongue to lap up blood.

UNIQUE MAMMAL
Bats are the only *mammals* (animals that feed their young on mother's milk) that can fly.

HOW BIG IS IT?

ON THE MOVE
Vampire bats can walk using their thumbs, while keeping their wings folded. They also jump well, an important ability for animals that must avoid being stepped on by cattle and other animals.

Indian Flying Fox

VITAL STATISTICS

WEIGHT	Females 1–2 lb (454–908 g); males 3–4 lb (1,361–1,816 g)
LENGTH	12 in (30 cm); wingspan is 4–5 ft (1.2–1.5 m)
SEXUAL MATURITY	1–2 years
LENGTH OF PREGNANCY	About 155 days
NUMBER OF OFFSPRING	1, occasionally 2; weaning occurs at 1 month
DIET	Feeds on such fruits as mango, guava, and banana; also eats pollen and nectar
LIFESPAN	Up to 15 years; can be 31 in captivity

ANIMAL FACTS

Flying foxes live in large colonies called camps. Several hundred bats may *roost* (perch) in a single tree, stripping off the leaves as they clamber around on the branches. At night, the bats leave the tree to feed. They do not rely on sound to navigate, as many other bats do. Their sharp night vision is enough. Youngsters are carried by their mother when she goes *foraging* (searching) for food, until they learn to fly at 11 weeks old.

The bat's wings can be used for swimming as well as flying.

Flying foxes, also known as "fruit bats," are the largest type of bat. Their name comes from their face, which resembles that of a fox. Farmers often kill flying foxes because they eat the fruit grown in orchards.

WHERE IN THE WORLD?

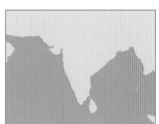

Found in India, Bangladesh, Pakistan, Myanmar (formerly known as Burma) and Sri Lanka, as well as the Maldives. Prefers areas of forest and swampland, usually near the coast.

WINGS
Broad and powerful, the wings allow the bat to cover long distances from its roost when seeking food.

COAT
Thick fur helps keep the bat warm.

HEAD
The fox-like shape of the head explains why these bats are called flying foxes.

EYES
The eyes are large, providing good night vision; flying foxes rely on their sight to fly in darkness.

HOW BIG IS IT?

HANGING ON
The hind feet each have five digits, which are equipped with sharp claws, so they can grasp branches when roosting.

Pygmy Anteater

SPECIES • *Cyclopes didactylus*

VITAL STATISTICS

WEIGHT	6–13 oz (175–357 g)
LENGTH	15–20 in (36–52 cm)
SEXUAL MATURITY	Probably about 1 year
LENGTH OF PREGNANCY	120–150 days; young are born in a tree hole lined with leaves
NUMBER OF OFFSPRING	1; weaning occurs at around 5 months
DIET	Feeds almost exclusively on ants, eating up to 8,000 per day
LIFESPAN	At least 2.5 years

The pygmy anteater is the smallest anteater in the world. It is also called the "silky anteater" because of its soft fur.

WHERE IN THE WORLD?

Lives in southern Mexico through Central America and the Amazon region in South America, reaching Brazil and remote parts of Bolivia and Peru.

ANIMAL FACTS

The pygmy anteater inhabits areas of heavy rain forest, moving easily from one tree to another. It rarely descends to the ground. It favors silk cotton trees, because the anteater resembles the tree's large seed pods. Thus, the tree offers excellent *camouflage* (disguise) for the animal. The anteater needs such protection, for it is at risk from harpy eagles and other birds of prey, which swoop down to seize it. The pygmy anteater feeds mainly on ants and termites that live in the treetops. It slurps up these insects with its long, sticky tongue.

The front feet (left) have two large claws, and the hind feet (right) have four claws.

COAT
The coat is golden brown with a paler underside. It has a dense texture.

FEET
The claws and *footpads* (pillowy structures on the bottoms of the feet) are large and help the anteater hold on to branches.

SLEEPING
Pygmy anteaters curl up in a ball in a tree to sleep during the day.

GRASPING TAIL
This acts like a hand, helping the anteater to grip branches.

LITTLE THREATS
When threatened, a pygmy anteater rears up on its hind legs, so that it appears larger, and lashes out with its claws. But the anteater rarely leaves the safety of the trees.

HOW BIG IS IT?

Pangolin

VITAL STATISTICS

WEIGHT	Ranges from 9 lb (4.1 kg) in the tree pangolin to 73 lb (33 kg) in the giant pangolin
LENGTH	3–5 ft (0.9–1.5 m)
SEXUAL MATURITY	2 years
LENGTH OF PREGNANCY	65–139 days; scales are soft in newborn pangolins
NUMBER OF OFFSPRING	Usually 1 but can be up to 3; weaning occurs at about 3 months
DIET	Feeds on ants and termites
LIFESPAN	Up to 20 years

ANIMAL FACTS

There are several *species* (kinds) of pangolins. Many are active at night. Their keen sense of smell enables them to locate nests of ants, which they break open with their sharp front claws. They use their tongues, which reach up to 16 inches (40 centimeters) long, to pull out the insects. Pangolins have a special *gland* (organ) that ensures their tongue remains sticky, trapping as many insects as possible. When threatened, pangolins roll up into a ball, exposing only their scaly armor to attackers.

The front legs of pangolins are relatively short.

The pangolin's name comes from the Malaysian word *pengguling,* which means *something that rolls up.* The pangolin is protected by a coat of armor formed by overlapping horny scales.

WHERE IN THE WORLD?

Found in Asia, from India east to China and south to Indonesia, and also across much of western and central Africa.

SCALES
This tough armor is made of keratin, the same material in human fingernails and hair.

FACE
Long and narrow, with no teeth but a long tongue in the mouth.

FRONT FEET
The front feet have long, sharp claws for breaking into the nests of ants and termites.

TAIL
Long and flexible, the tail is well protected by scales.

LIFESTYLE
While some pangolins live in trees, others *burrow* (dig) into the ground, up to 11 feet (3.5 meters) below the surface.

HOW BIG IS IT?

GRASPING TAIL
Many pangolins can use their tail to grasp branches and support their weight.

Hoffman's Two-Toed Sloth

SPECIES • *Choloepus hoffmanni*

VITAL STATISTICS

WEIGHT	9–18 lb (4–8 kg)
LENGTH	23–28 in (58–70 cm)
SEXUAL MATURITY	Females 3 years; males 4–5 years
LENGTH OF PREGNANCY	Up to 365 days
NUMBER OF OFFSPRING	1; weaning occurs at 1 month; the youngster remains with its mother for 2–3 months
DIET	Feeds on fruit, berries, bark, and other plant matter; also eggs and rodents
LIFESPAN	12 years; up to 31 in captivity

ANIMAL FACTS

Sloths move very slowly through the treetops. They almost never visit the ground, where their slow speed makes them vulnerable to *predators* (hunting animals). Sloths live in a moist environment, which encourages the growth of *algae* (simple plant-like organisms) in their fur. As a result, the fur of many sloths has a greenish-brown color. Sloths eat large amounts of plant matter, which can take up to a month to pass through their digestive system.

Sloths spend most of their lives hanging upside down from branches. Special muscles in the limbs of sloths enable them to hang without conscious effort. As a result, they can even sleep upside down.

WHERE IN THE WORLD?

Lives in Central and South America, from Nicaragua down to Peru, Bolivia, and Brazil. It is most common in Panama.

HANGING AROUND
Sloths hang so well from branches that they may remain in the trees for some time after they have died.

A RESTFUL EXISTENCE
Much of the sloth's time is spent resting, hanging off branches.

CLAWS
As its name suggests, this animal has just two claws on its front feet. It has three claws on its hind feet.

COLORATION
The body is dark, contrasting with the face. The underside is also paler.

SNOUT
This is relatively pronounced, with large nostrils.

SLICING AND DICING
If unfortunate enough to be caught on the ground, a sloth will try to protect itself using its sharp claws.

HOW BIG IS IT?

Pads behind the claws help the sloth to maintain its grip.

Flying Lemur

VITAL STATISTICS

WEIGHT	2–4 lb (1–2 kg)
LENGTH	13–15 in (33–38 cm)
SEXUAL MATURITY	About 3 years
LENGTH OF PREGNANCY	60 days; young are born in a very immature state
NUMBER OF OFFSPRING	1; weaning occurs from 6 months
DIET	Feeds mainly on leaves and flowers, as well as sap; may also eat fruit
LIFESPAN	Up to 15 years

ANIMAL FACTS

Flying lemurs avoid danger on the forest floor by staying in the trees as much as possible. They glide from tree to tree to find fresh leaves to eat. Large folds of skin on the animal's sides connect its neck, legs, and tail. When it spreads its legs, this skin forms "wings" used for gliding. Although flying lemurs are not *marsupials* (animals that carry young in a pouch), they give birth to tiny young that weigh only 1.2 ounces (35 grams). The mother carries her young on the underside of her body for six months. Flying lemurs are hunted for their meat.

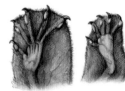

The flying lemur's gliding membrane extends between the individual toes.

Flying lemurs are poorly named, for they are not true lemurs. They also cannot fly, though they open folds of skin to make "wings" to glide between trees. These mammals are also known as "colugos."

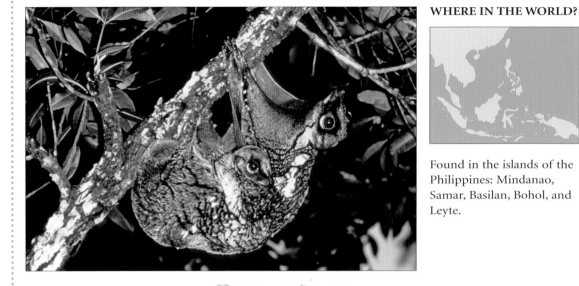

WHERE IN THE WORLD?

Found in the islands of the Philippines: Mindanao, Samar, Basilan, Bohol, and Leyte.

FEET
The absence of a thumb makes it more difficult for these animals to climb.

GLIDING MEMBRANE
This membrane is kept folded away while the flying lemur is resting on a tree.

CLAWS
Flying lemurs hop up branches, using their sharp claws to anchor themselves.

EYES
Keen eyesight enables the flying lemur to land safely on another tree.

TEETH
The animal's teeth look something like combs, with as many as 20 lines on each.

HOW BIG IS IT?

GLIDING ABILITY
Flying lemurs can travel up to 230 feet (70 meters) by gliding, much as people use hang gliders to soar on air currents.

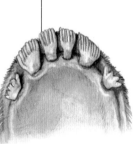

Ring-Tailed Lemur

SPECIES • *Lemur catta*

VITAL STATISTICS

WEIGHT	5.1–7.7 lb (2.3–3.5 kg)
LENGTH	15–17 in (38–45 cm); tail is about 22 in (55 cm)
SEXUAL MATURITY	2.5–3 years
LENGTH OF PREGNANCY	About 135 days
NUMBER OF OFFSPRING	1, very rarely twins; weaning occurs by 5 months
DIET	Eats fruits and leaves; also flowers, nuts, and insects
LIFESPAN	Up to 19 years; 27 years in captivity

ANIMAL FACTS

Lemurs live in small groups that defend a *territory* (personal area). The groups are led by females that help one another raise their young. These *mammals* (animals that feed their young on mother's milk) often sunbathe before they move into the trees to feed. Lemurs are eaten mainly by the fossa, a tree-dwelling, cat-like animal. People also hunt lemurs. But the main threat to lemurs is the loss of their forest *habitat* (living place). As forests in Madagascar have been cut down, the number of ring-tailed lemurs has fallen greatly.

Lemurs have highly specialized hands, with a sharp claw on each front foot for *grooming* (washing and brushing the coat).

Lemurs are *primates,* the group to which monkeys, apes, and human beings belong. Lemurs live only on Madagascar. Their ancestors reached the island from Africa about 45 million to 65 million years ago.

WHERE IN THE WORLD?

Found only on the island of Madagascar, off the southeastern coast of Africa, mainly in southern and southwestern areas.

EYES
The bright yellow or orange eyes are surrounded by black rings of fur.

COAT
The dense fur is gray on the back and paler on the underside.

HIND LEGS
These are longer than the front legs, as they are in other lemur *species* (kinds).

TAIL
Alternating black and white bands run down the tail, which ends in a black tip.

TAIL TALK
The tail cannot grasp branches, but it is used for balance and communication among lemurs.

HOW BIG IS IT?

ON THE GROUND

Ring-tailed lemurs spend more time on the ground than most other lemurs, and they sometimes travel across the ground in groups.

Indri Lemur

VITAL STATISTICS

WEIGHT	15–22 lb (7–10 kg); males are slightly larger
LENGTH	About 28 in (71 cm)
SEXUAL MATURITY	7–9 years for both sexes
LENGTH OF PREGNANCY	120–150 days
NUMBER OF OFFSPRING	1; weaning occurs at around 6 months
DIET	Mainly fruit, but also leaves and other plant matter, including flowers
LIFESPAN	Probably up to 40 years

ANIMAL FACTS

Indri are the largest of all lemurs. They spend nearly all of their time in the trees. Their toes are fused together, except for the big toe. This feature helps them to jump from branch to branch. When these lemurs come down to the ground, they move in much the same way, jumping and holding their long arms above their head. Pairs are active during the day, and mark their *territory* (personal area) with urine. Like many other animals of Madagascar, indri lemurs are endangered. Much of the forest where they live has been cut down.

The wailing call of this lemur carries far through the forest.

This animal's name originates in a misunderstanding. A local person showing the lemur to a visitor declared, "Indri," which means *there it is.* The visitor thought *indri* was the name of the lemur.

WHERE IN THE WORLD?

Found only on the island of Madagascar, in north-eastern forests.

HITCHING A RIDE
A young indri lemur clings to its mother's belly for five months, before moving to her back for another two months.

BIG TOE
This is much larger than the thumb, helping the lemur to grasp branches.

EARS
These are set quite low on the head and have a distinctive tufted appearance.

COLORATION
The indri's coat varies markedly. Black areas may be replaced by brown or even gray.

TAIL
The tiny tail measures only about 2.4 inches (6 centimeters) long.

HOW BIG IS IT?

GROOMING
Lemurs groom one another to bond and build social ties.

Brown Howler Monkey

SPECIES • *Alouatta guariba*

These monkeys are named for their loud calls. Their grunts and barks travel through the forest, marking their *territories* (personal areas). The sounds warn neighboring troops of monkeys not to trespass.

VITAL STATISTICS

WEIGHT	9–15 lb (4–7 kg); females are smaller
LENGTH	37–50 in (93–126 cm) overall; the tail is slightly longer than the body
SEXUAL MATURITY	Females 3 years; males 3.5 years
LENGTH OF PREGNANCY	About 190 days
NUMBER OF OFFSPRING	1; weaning occurs at 12–13 months; females give birth every 1.5–2 years
DIET	Mainly leaves but also fruit and other plant matter
LIFESPAN	Up to 20 years

ANIMAL FACTS

These are among the largest monkeys of Central and South America. Like many other *New World* (Western Hemisphere) monkeys, the brown howler monkey has a grasping tail. This tail helps to support its movements through the treetops. The calls of these monkeys do not simply mark a territory. They also enable nearby monkeys to estimate the size of the group, based on the variety of calls. In this way, the calls help to prevent confrontations between rival groups. Much of the brown howler monkey's forest *habitat* (living place) has been destroyed. It survives in the fragments that remain, but its numbers are falling.

WHERE IN THE WORLD?

Lives in South America, in southeastern Brazil and northeastern Argentina. May also be found in nearby areas of Uruguay and Bolivia.

FACE
This is free of fur, allowing the monkeys to use facial expressions to communicate.

HOWLING
In addition to marking territory, howling sounds the alarm about ocelots and other *predators* (hunting animals).

MANE
The fur is longer around the face, creating the appearance of a beard.

HANDS
The hands have five fingers, with the first finger and thumb opposite the other three.

SOUNDING OFF
There are often several males in a troop. Disputes between males are rare but males and females sometimes fight.

HOW BIG IS IT?

TAKING IT EASY

When they are not feeding, howler monkeys spend most of their time resting in the treetops. The leaves these monkeys eat provide relatively poor nutrition. As a result, howlers usually save energy by lounging for long periods.

Pygmy Marmoset

VITAL STATISTICS

WEIGHT	5–7 oz (150–200 g); females are smaller
LENGTH	5.5–6.25 in (14–16 cm); tail is 6-17 in (15–42 cm)
SEXUAL MATURITY	1–1.5 years
LENGTH OF PREGNANCY	119–140 days
NUMBER OF OFFSPRING	2, occasionally 3; males are responsible for carrying the young for 2 months, until they are largely weaned
DIET	Sap from trees; also eats insects and spiders
LIFESPAN	Up to 11 years

ANIMAL FACTS

This monkey uses its teeth in an unusual way, cutting notches in the bark of trees so it can feed on sap. This sap attracts insects, which the monkeys also eats. Pygmy marmosets live in small groups made up of an adult pair and their young. The monkeys are vocal, uttering a series of whistles, squeaks, and clicks. These calls enable them to communicate any hint of danger. At close quarters, they also communicate by means of facial gestures and body posture.

Facial gestures are used to communicate.

The pygmy marmoset is the smallest of all monkeys. Its lightness and its grace among the branches enable this monkey to feed off slender branches that are out of the reach of its heavier relatives.

WHERE IN THE WORLD?

Found in northern South America, restricted to the rain forest areas of southeastern Colombia, eastern parts of Ecuador and Peru, northern Bolivia, and western Brazil.

FACE
The face is broad, with the eyes close together and the ears hidden by fur.

ACROBATIC HUNTING
The pygmy marmoset's grace in the trees helps it to catch insects. It can jump up to 16 feet (5 meters) in a single bound.

LEGS AND FEET
Nimble and graceful, these marmosets easily run up and down branches.

COLORATION
The brownish-yellow patterning of their coat helps these monkeys hide among sun-dappled leaves.

TAIL
Long and slender, the tail is banded along its length and tapers to a tip. It cannot grasp branches.

HOW BIG IS IT?

DANGER ABOVE
Large snakes hunt pygmy marmosets, as do wildcats. The monkeys are also vulnerable to birds of prey that fly above the trees.

Golden Lion Tamarin

The golden lion tamarin is a striking monkey. The name "golden lion" comes from the monkey's color and the mane of hair around its face. Tamarins are monkeys of Central and South America.

VITAL STATISTICS

WEIGHT	14–30 oz (400–800 g)
LENGTH	18–22 in (45–56 cm) overall; the tail is longer than the body
SEXUAL MATURITY	Females 24 months; males 18 months
LENGTH OF PREGNANCY	About 130 days; young are born from September to March
NUMBER OF OFFSPRING	1; weaning occurs at 3–5 months; females give birth every 1.5–2 years
DIET	Fruit, insects, and other small animals
LIFESPAN	Up to 15 years; 28 in captivity

ANIMAL FACTS

The golden lion tamarin had nearly disappeared from the wild by the 1980's, with as few as 100 surviving. A major conservation effort, in cluding a breeding program in zoos, has increased the population to more than 1,000. Still, the monkeys remain *endangered* (at risk of dying out). They are threatened mainly by the destruction of their forest *habitat* (living place). Tamarins live in family groups. Juveniles help to raise newborns and learn parenting skills.

Strong bonds exist between members of the group.

WHERE IN THE WORLD?

Lives in coastal areas of Brazil, in Rio de Janeiro and Espirito Santos states.

HITCHING A RIDE
Young tamarins ride on the back of an adult, usually the male.

MANE
In both sexes, a long mane of fur surrounds the dark-colored face.

FEET
Long toes help the monkey to grasp branches.

CLAWS
Monkeys generally have nails instead of claws. The nails are useful for grabbing insects.

HOW BIG IS IT?

HAVE A SEAT

The tamarin typically rests on its haunches, using its hands to collect food. In addition to plant matter, the monkey eats insects, spiders, snails, birds, lizards, and eggs.

White-Faced Capuchin Monkey

SPECIES • *Cebus capucinus*

White-faced capuchins live in groups of 20 to 30 monkeys. They are energetic and inquisitive. These monkeys, also known as "sapajous," spend much of their time playing in the treetops.

VITAL STATISTICS

WEIGHT	6–12 lb (2.6–5.5 kg); males are heavier
LENGTH	29–38 in (74–96 cm) overall; tail is longer than the body
SEXUAL MATURITY	5–6 years
LENGTH OF PREGNANCY	About 150 days; births coincide with the wet season
NUMBER OF OFFSPRING	1; twins are rare; weaning takes place by 2 years
DIET	Eats mainly fruit; also other plant matter, insects, and small animals
LIFESPAN	Up to 30 years in the wild

ANIMAL FACTS

Capuchins communicate through a variety of gestures and calls. A trilling call warns the group that a *predator* (hunting animal) has been spotted. Tree snakes are the greatest danger, though wildcats and birds of prey are also threats. Capuchins regularly *groom* (wash and brush the coat of) one another and play games that help them to form strong social bonds. There are several *species* (kinds) of capuchins.

These monkeys are named after the Capuchin friars, a Catholic religious order. The black fur on their head is said to resemble a monk's hood.

WHERE IN THE WORLD?

Range extends from Hondurus in Central America into South America, where they can be found in parts of Colombia and Ecuador.

TAIL
This can grasp branches, freeing the other limbs to do such tasks as collecting food.

FUR
The thick fur is mostly black, with some white on the arms, chest, and face.

FACIAL FEATURES
The skin on the face is tan to pink, and the surrounding fur is white.

EARS
These are relatively large and flattened on the sides of the head. They are not hidden by hair.

HOW BIG IS IT?

FOOD AND DRINK
Capuchins may drink by using their hands to scoop up water. They come down to the ground to collect fruit.

Vervet Monkey

SPECIES • *Chlorocebus pygerythrus*

VITAL STATISTICS

WEIGHT	5–10 lb (2.5–4.5 kg); males are heavier
LENGTH	25–37 in (64–93 cm) overall; tail is usually longer than the body
SEXUAL MATURITY	4–6 years
LENGTH OF PREGNANCY	About 210 days; births coincide with the start of the wet season
NUMBER OF OFFSPRING	1; weaning occurs from 6 months
DIET	Feeds mainly on fruit; also other plant matter, insects, and small animals
LIFESPAN	Up to 20 years

ANIMAL FACTS

Vervet monkeys usually live in relatively open forest. They can *adapt* (adjust) to various environments, including cities. They may gather food either on the ground or in the trees. They live in troops of up to 80 individuals. Vervets are vocal but also communicate by facial gestures. In some areas, people regard vervets as pests because they feed on crops. The monkeys have also been used in medical research.

Wildcats prey on vervets, but the monkeys are difficult to catch in the trees.

Vervet monkeys use warning calls to alert other members of their troop to the approach of *predators* (hunting animals). They use different alarms to identify eagles, leopards, and snakes.

WHERE IN THE WORLD?

Lives in southeastern and southern Africa. Also introduced to the Caribbean islands of Barbados and Saint Kitts.

VERVET
The slight greenish tinge to the fur explains why they are called vervets, from the French word *vert*, which means *green*.

TAIL
The tail cannot grasp branches but is used for balance and communication.

FAMILY TREE
Vervets belong to the guenon group of monkeys. Vervets are probably the most common *species* (kind) of monkey in Africa.

HANDS
The hands, like the feet, are black and similar to human hands in structure.

FAMILY TIES
Females help one another raise the young. They discipline young who behave badly, such as those who deliberately use the wrong predator call in order to tease the adults.

HOW BIG IS IT?

Mandrill

VITAL STATISTICS

WEIGHT	25–90 lb (11–40 kg); males weigh twice as much as females
LENGTH	25–35 in (63–88 cm), including short tail
SEXUAL MATURITY	Females 3.5 years; males 4.5–7 years
LENGTH OF PREGNANCY	About 186 days
NUMBER OF OFFSPRING	1, rarely twins; weaning occurs at around 8 months
DIET	Eats fruit, leaves, seeds, nuts, roots, and insects
LIFESPAN	Up to 46 years

ANIMAL FACTS

Mandrills resemble baboons, having long arms, small pig-like eyes, large *canine* (biting) teeth, and a muzzle similar to that of a dog. Like most other monkeys, mandrills live in groups, which range from 15 to 95 individuals. Males protect the group against leopards and other threats. Mandrills move about on the ground and in trees. Females carry their young slung beneath their bodies. Mandrill numbers have fallen because of hunting.

Mandrills have formidable canine teeth that measure up to 2 inches (5 centimeters) long.

Mandrills are among the largest, most colorful monkeys. The male is especially colorful. Its cheeks are blue; its long, flat nose is red; and its rump is red and blue.

WHERE IN THE WORLD?

Lives in western Africa, in southwestern Cameroon, western Gabon, Equatorial Guinea, and southwestern Republic of the Congo.

SIZE
Male mandrills often weigh twice as much as females.

CHANGE IN APPEARANCE
The skin color becomes brighter when the monkey is excited.

FUR
This is mainly olive-brown, with a whitish underside.

COLORATION
The color of the mandrill's distinctive rump may help the monkeys to see each other in the forest.

HOW BIG IS IT?

CHANGING APPEARANCE
Young mandrills have predominantly dark faces. They start to develop their distinctive coloration as they grow older. Males are more colorful than females.

Proboscis Monkey

VITAL STATISTICS

WEIGHT	25–50 lb (12–24 kg); males may weigh twice as much as females
LENGTH	55–60 in (135–147 cm) overall; tail is longer than the body
SEXUAL MATURITY	Females 4 years; males 4–7 years
LENGTH OF PREGNANCY	166 days
NUMBER OF OFFSPRING	1; weaning occurs at around 8 months
DIET	Eats mainly leaves; also fruits, seeds, and insects
LIFESPAN	Up to 23 years

The male's nose gives these monkeys their name, for the word *proboscis* is a humorous name for a long nose. Proboscis monkeys live in trees along the coasts or near rivers.

WHERE IN THE WORLD?

Found only in Southeast Asia, on the island of Borneo.

ANIMAL FACTS

Proboscis monkeys prefer mangrove forests along the coasts. The monkeys wade upright in the shallows. They can also swim well and drop off branches into the water to escape such *predators* (hunting animals) as clouded leopards. However, the monkeys are sometimes eaten by crocodiles lurking in the water. Proboscis monkeys have become endangered, mainly because people have cut down their forest *habitats* (living places).

NOSE
Up to 7 inches (18 centimeters) long, this swells with blood if the male feels threatened.

HANDS
These monkeys use their hands to pick young leaves from the trees.

TOES
Webbing between the toes helps these monkeys to swim.

BELLY
Large and rounded, the *chambered* (divided) stomach houses *microbes* (germs) to break down vegetation.

Even when drinking, proboscis monkeys rarely descend to the ground.

HOW BIG IS IT?

NOSE APPEAL
The large nose of the male (foreground) makes him attractive to the female. The nose also makes his calls louder. One male typically breeds with several females.

Gorilla

VITAL STATISTICS

WEIGHT	150–400 lb (68–177 kg); males are larger
LENGTH	4–6 ft (1.2–1.8 m)
SEXUAL MATURITY	Females 10 years; males 15 years
LENGTH OF PREGNANCY	251–289 days
NUMBER OF OFFSPRING	1, very rarely twins; weaning occurs at 3–4 years
DIET	Feeds mainly on leaves; also fruit, flowers, roots, and some insects
LIFESPAN	Up to 50 years

The gorilla is the largest of the apes. A large male gorilla living in the wild may weigh 390 pounds (177 kilograms) and stand 6 feet (1.8 meters) tall. Gorillas are among the most intelligent animals.

WHERE IN THE WORLD?

Western Africa, living in Gabon, Equatorial Guinea, Central African Republic, Democratic Republic of the Congo, Cameroon, and south as far as Angola.

ANIMAL FACTS

A gorilla that feels threatened may stand up and beat its chest. But gorillas are generally peaceful and shy. They live in small family groups that move through their *territory* (personal area). They make fresh grass nests each night. They may climb trees to reach fruit, especially the younger members of the group. Gorillas are highly *endangered* (at risk of dying out) in the wild. They face a variety of threats, including *poaching* (illegal hunting), human warfare, loss of forest *habitat* (living places), and disease.

HEAD COLORATION
The reddish area on the head is a distinctive feature of lowland gorillas.

FEET
These are broad to support walking, but the big toe is widely spaced to support climbing.

FOREARMS
These are strong. Gorillas walk on their knuckles rather than on their palms.

FEMALES
Females lack the silver fur on the back that characterizes powerful males.

Male gorillas appear especially formidable when they stand and beat their chests.

HOW BIG IS IT?

FEEDING

Gorillas may venture into wet areas to feed on water plants. Gorillas have been seen using walking sticks in swampy areas. Thus, gorillas are among the few animals that use simple tools.

Bornean Orangutan

VITAL STATISTICS

WEIGHT	75–180 lb (33–82 kg); males are larger
LENGTH	4–5 ft (1.2–1.5 cm)
SEXUAL MATURITY	15 years for both sexes
LENGTH OF PREGNANCY	About 260 days; females are pregnant only once every 8 years
NUMBER OF OFFSPRING	1, rarely twins; weaning occurs at 3.5–4.5 years
DIET	Eats mainly fruit; also leaves, bark, and insects
LIFESPAN	Up to 60 years

The word *orangutan* means *person of the forest*. These apes are the largest *mammals* (animals whose young feed on their mother's milk) that live among the treetops, only rarely coming down to the ground.

WHERE IN THE WORLD?

Lives only on the island of Borneo in Southeast Asia.

ANIMAL FACTS

Orangutans are less social than other apes. Adults live far apart in the forest and usually avoid one another. The apes are intelligent and can make simple tools from sticks and leaves. They use these tools as probes, sponges, and umbrellas. These apes are *endangered* (at risk of dying out), mainly because their forests have been cut down and replaced by oil palm plantations. Female orangutans are hunted so their young can be collected for the wildlife trade. The closely related Sumatran orangutan is also endangered.

The feet are well suited to grasping branches and vines.

FACE
Males often have broad, flat cheek pads called *flanges* around the face, along with a flap under the throat.

COAT
The coats of these great apes are shaggy and reddish.

ARMS
These may reach about 6 feet (2 meters) long. The hands are largely free of fur.

HOW BIG IS IT?

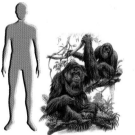

ON THE MOVE
Orangutans use both their arms and legs together to grasp branches as they swing through the forest. They are more graceful in the trees than on the ground.

Chimpanzee

VITAL STATISTICS

WEIGHT	65–130 lb (30–60 kg); males are larger
LENGTH	3.25–5.5 ft (100–170 cm)
SEXUAL MATURITY	13–15 years for both sexes
LENGTH OF PREGNANCY	About 230 days
NUMBER OF OFFSPRING	1, rarely twins; weaning occurs at 3.5–4.5 years
DIET	Feeds on fruit, leaves, and other plant matter; also insects, monkeys, and small animals
LIFESPAN	Up to 60 years

ANIMAL FACTS

Chimpanzees are highly social, living in groups that occupy *territories* (personal areas). They are skilled hunters, often working together to trap monkeys and other animals. Bands of chimps may also attack chimps in rival bands to seize their territory. Chimps are *endangered* (at risk of dying out) in the wild. They are threatened by *poaching* (illegal hunting), the loss of their forest *habitat* (living place), and disease.

When young chimpanzees play together, they laugh much like human children.

Chimpanzees are closely related to human beings and share many of our characteristics. Chimps are intelligent, playful, and curious. They live both in trees and on the ground.

WHERE IN THE WORLD?

Found in western and central Africa, from Gambia across to the Democratic Republic of the Congo and east to Uganda.

MOTHER LOVE

The females raise their young by themselves. The infants ride under the mother's body, supported by her arm, until they are about 5 months old. Then they ride on the mother's back. Young chimps stay with their mother until they are about 6 years old.

HANDS

Like other great apes, chimps are skilled with their hands. They also use tools, including sticks to collect termites and rocks to break open nuts.

COLORATION

The skin of chimpanzees darkens with age, though their hair often becomes grayish over the back.

HOW BIG IS IT?

CHIMP COMMOTION

Chimpanzees communicate through barks, grunts, and screams. When they find food, the apes jump, hoot loudly, and beat on tree trunks.

Bonobo

VITAL STATISTICS

WEIGHT	70–100 lb (32–45 kg); males are larger
LENGTH	41–49 in (104–124 cm)
SEXUAL MATURITY	13–15 years for both sexes
LENGTH OF PREGNANCY	About 240 days
NUMBER OF OFFSPRING	1, very rarely twins; weaning occurs at 4 years
DIET	Eats mainly fruit; also leaves, other plant matter, insects; rarely, small animals
LIFESPAN	Up to 50 years

ANIMAL FACTS

Bonobos and chimps are the closest living relatives of human beings. Bonobos are cousins to chimps, and they are similar in most respects. The biggest differences are in behavior. Female chimps are often harassed by male chimps. In contrast, bonobo females form strong relationships that protect them from being overpowered by males. Partly as a result, there appears to be less violence among bonobos than there is among chimps. Bonobos are *endangered* (at risk of dying out). Like chimps, they face *poaching* (illegal hunting), the loss of their forest *habitat* (living place), and disease.

The longer-legged, somewhat slimmer bonobo (left) is similar in appearance to the chimpanzee (right).

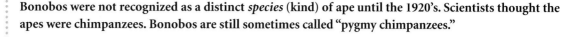

Bonobos were not recognized as a distinct *species* (kind) of ape until the 1920's. Scientists thought the apes were chimpanzees. Bonobos are still sometimes called "pygmy chimpanzees."

WHERE IN THE WORLD?

Lives in forests in the Democratic Republic of the Congo, occupying an area between the Congo and Lualaba rivers, south to the Kasai River.

NOT CHIMPS
Bonobos have smaller heads, flatter faces, and longer legs than chimpanzees do.

HIND LEGS
These are relatively long, with distinctive knees. Bonobos appear to walk upright more often than other apes, especially when they are carrying a burden.

HAIR
This is black and clearly apparent on the cheeks. The skin is also dark in color.

KNUCKLE WALKERS
Like chimps and gorillas, bonobos usually walk on their knuckles.

DAILY LIFE
Finding food occupies a large amount of the bonobo's day.

HOW BIG IS IT?

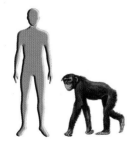

TOOL USE
Like other great apes, bonobos use simple tools. In this case, the bonobo has rolled up a leaf to collect and drink water.

Indian Gray Mongoose

SPECIES • *Herpestes edwardsii*

VITAL STATISTICS

WEIGHT	2–4 lb (0.9–1.7 kg); males are larger
LENGTH	31–36 in (80–91 cm), including tail
SEXUAL MATURITY	6–9 months
LENGTH OF PREGNANCY	60–65 days
NUMBER OF OFFSPRING	Average 2–5; weaning occurs at around 180 days
DIET	Eats mainly snakes, lizards, rodents, insects, birds, fruit, and roots
LIFESPAN	7–9 years in the wild; up to 11 in captivity

ANIMAL FACTS

The mongoose is totally without fear. It will confront a large king cobra and avoid its strikes for an hour or more. Then, it will bite the snake on the neck. The little *mammal* (animal who feeds its young on the mother's milk) also feeds on scorpions. Again, quickness is key. The mongoose grabs the scorpion and throws it against rocks before it can sting. In fact, mongooses eat many different kinds of foods. They climb trees to raid bird nests. Their hunger for bird eggs sometimes gets them into trouble with farmers, who may regard the mongoose as a pest. But the mongoose helps to control the numbers of rodents and snakes.

The mongoose is a terror to even the deadliest snakes. The animal moves so quickly and gracefully that it can evade a striking cobra until the snake is exhausted. The mongoose then moves in for the kill.

WHERE IN THE WORLD?

Lives mainly in India, but also found in parts of Saudi Arabia, Iran, Pakistan, Bangladesh, and Sri Lanka.

COAT TEXTURE
The hairs along the back are much coarser than those elsewhere on the body.

HEAD
Mongooses have broad jaws and small ears. The head merges into the neck.

TAIL
The tail is about as long as the rest of the body.

COLORATION
In spite of their name, these mongooses range in color from gray to tawny-red.

HOW BIG IS IT?

HIDING AWAY
When it is not hunting, a mongoose hides in a *burrow* (underground shelter). The burrow protects it from the heat of the day as well as from leopards, which eat mongooses.

King Cobra

VITAL STATISTICS

WEIGHT	Up to 20 lb (9 kg)
LENGTH	Typically 12–13 ft (3.6–4 m), but can reach 18 ft (5.5 m)
SEXUAL MATURITY	2 years
NUMBER OF EGGS	3–12, laid underground or in hollow logs in summer
INCUBATION PERIOD	About 3 months; young are dangerous as soon as they hatch
DIET	Eats mainly snakes; also lizards and small animals
LIFESPAN	Up to 20 years

The king cobra is the largest *venomous* (poisonous) snake in the world. It can reach lengths up to 18 feet (5.5 meters), though most are smaller.

WHERE IN THE WORLD?

Lives in northern and eastern India, through southern China and into Southeast Asia, including the islands of Indonesia and the Philippines.

ANIMAL FACTS

The venom of the king cobra works by blocking nerve signals, which prevents the victim from breathing. The venom is so deadly that it can kill an adult elephant in a few hours. Fortunately, the snakes usually avoid contact with people and slither away rather than attack. Still, king cobras bite and sometimes kill people. Victims must be treated with *antivenin,* which neutralizes venom. However, people in remote areas may not be able to get treatment in time. King cobras are unusual among snakes in that they build a nest and guard their eggs. Females are fierce when defending the nest. Despite their fearsome nature, cobras are threatened, both by loss of their forest *habitat* (living place) and hunting by people. The number of these snakes has fallen.

JAWS
The jaws are quite flexible, allowing the snake to swallow prey much larger than its head.

POSTURE
If threatened, the snake raises its head, which enables it to track a threat and strike from a distance.

HOOD
A cobra can flatten its neck to extend the hood. The hood helps the snake look more menacing.

COLORATION
The back is blackish, with a paler underside.

BLENDING IN
Camouflage (disguise) helps the snake to blend in with leaf litter and vegetation on the forest floor.

HOW BIG IS IT?

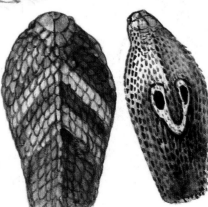

A DRAMATIC SIGHT
The rear of the hood has a striking pattern of *ocelli,* or false eyes, which may confuse an attacker.

Boa Constrictor

VITAL STATISTICS

WEIGHT	Up to 60 lb (27 kg)
LENGTH	10–14 ft (3–4.3 m) on average
SEXUAL MATURITY	2–4 years
INCUBATION PERIOD	100–150 days; eggs develop and hatch inside the mother's body, and young are born live
NUMBER OF OFFSPRING	20–50
DIET	Eats mainly bats, birds, and rodents
LIFESPAN	10–30 years

ANIMAL FACTS

Boa constrictors are great hunters of the forest. They often hunt in the trees, seizing bats and birds. Older, larger boas may spend more time on the ground. Their coloration helps them to hide in leaf litter on the forest floor. In this way, they are able to ambush prey. They also are at home in the water. After a large meal, they may become inactive for a week while they digest their food. They can go for months without eating. Unlike most reptiles, boas give birth to live young. The eggs develop inside the mother's body and hatch before birth.

Boas often hunt bats at night.

Boa constrictors hunt mainly in the trees. Like other constrictors, boas kill prey by suffocation, grasping their victim so tightly that it cannot breathe.

WHERE IN THE WORLD?

Found over a wide area, from northern Mexico through Central and South America, as well as various Caribbean islands.

COLORATION
Variable through the boa constrictor's wide range. The tail is often reddish.

COILS
Boas can move along the top of a branch and also grasp it with their coils to hang off the side.

JAWS
Boas kill with their coils, but when threatened, they strike and bite. They lack fangs but have many backward facing teeth.

TONGUE
Forked at the tip, the tongue helps to collect scents, both from prey and potential mates.

HOW BIG IS IT?

MATING
This often occurs on the ground. Females attract males with a special scent.

Indian Python

These large constrictors are kept as pets, but young snakes soon grow to great size. They may reach up to 21 feet (6 meters) long and weigh as much as 200 pounds (91 kilograms).

VITAL STATISTICS

WEIGHT	Up to 200 lb (91 kg)
LENGTH	Can reach 21 ft (6 m)
SEXUAL MATURITY	3 years
NUMBER OF EGGS	20–60, can be up to 100
INCUBATION PERIOD	2–3 months
DIET	Eats a variety of animals, including rodents, birds, amphibians, and reptiles
LIFESPAN	20–30 years

ANIMAL FACTS

Indian pythons are ambush hunters, striking from the forest floor. A constrictor, the snake wraps itself around its victim. After the animal stops breathing, the snake swallows it, headfirst. A *subspecies* (variety) of this snake is known as the Burmese python. Thousands of these snakes now live in Florida. Most are descended from boas released into the wild after they grew too large for the people who had bought them as pets. These snakes are now spreading out of control, partly because they lay many eggs and hide well. They have done great damage in the Everglades by feeding on native wildlife. However, their numbers are falling in their native Asia.

Like other snakes, pythons regularly shed their skin as they grow, a process called *molting*.

WHERE IN THE WORLD?

Lives in southern Asia, in India, Sri Lanka, Pakistan, and Nepal. Introduced to the United States in Florida.

TAIL
The body tapers along its length and the tail is narrow.

PATTERNING
This is highly individual and provides excellent *camouflage* (disguise) for the snakes when on the ground.

ON THEIR OWN
Young pythons set off on their own soon after they hatch, and the female plays no further part in their care.

CLIMBING
Young Indian pythons often climb trees, but heavier, older individuals rarely leave the ground.

PITS
Pits along the upper lip detect heat, enabling the snake to "see" prey in total darkness.

HOW BIG IS IT?

MATERNAL INSTINCTS
The female python curls around her eggs, keeping them warm with body heat, which she increases by shivering her muscles. She may not eat until after the eggs have hatched.

Komodo Dragon

VITAL STATISTICS

WEIGHT	Up to 365 lb (166 kg)
LENGTH	Can be more than 10 ft (3 m)
SEXUAL MATURITY	Females 6–9 years; males 7–10 years
NUMBER OF EGGS	15–30
INCUBATION PERIOD	8 months; hatchlings measure only 16 in (40 cm) long
DIET	Eats mainly animal remains; also hunts deer, goats, pigs, and other animals
LIFESPAN	30–50 years

ANIMAL FACTS

The Komodo dragon relies on its sharp sense of smell to find animal remains. It can detect scents from more than 2 miles (3.2 kilometers) away. It also ambushes living prey, using its large, *serrated* (notched) teeth to tear away hunks of flesh. The lizard then waits for the injured animal to die from blood loss or infection. The saliva of the dragon is filled with bacteria, and a bite can quickly cause blood poisoning. The saliva also carries *venom* (poison). Young dragons live in trees, mainly to avoid being eaten by older dragons. Komodo dragons are *threatened* (in danger of dying out). Fewer than 5,000 survive in the wild.

The curved claws of the Komodo dragon can inflict serious injury.

The Komodo dragon is the largest living lizard, reaching more than 10 feet (3 meters) long. It can take down prey as large as horses and water buffaloes. It has even attacked and eaten human beings.

WHERE IN THE WORLD?

Only on the Indonesian islands of Komodo and Flores in southeastern Asia.

TONGUE
The long, forked tongue gathers scents, helping the lizard to find animal remains.

TAIL
The powerful tail can be used to strike other animals. It also helps the lizard to swim.

LEGS
Powerful legs are equipped with claws to assist in climbing.

FIGHTING

Males fight over females by wrestling in an upright position. The males bite each other, but they do not develop infections from the bites. Scientists do not know how the lizards resist infection.

HOW BIG IS IT?

BALANCE
The tail supports the body when standing.

Frilled Lizard

VITAL STATISTICS

WEIGHT	About 1 lb (0.5 kg)
LENGTH	28–38 in (70–95 cm), including the tail
SEXUAL MATURITY	2–2.5 years
NUMBER OF EGGS	8–23, with some females laying twice per season
INCUBATION PERIOD	2–3 months; young weigh 0.1–0.18 oz (3–5 g)
DIET	Eats mainly insects, both in the trees and on the ground
LIFESPAN	12–15 years

ANIMAL FACTS

The frilled lizard spends most of its time in the trees. It is a strong climber, and its long tail provides balance. The lizard's frill makes it appear larger, to frighten attackers. The frill also has other uses. Raising or lowering the frill can help the lizard control its body temperature. The frill is also important in courtship displays, when males try to impress females. When the lizard comes down to the ground, it can run on its hind legs. The number of these lizards has fallen. They are *threatened* (in danger of dying out) by loss of *habitat* (living place), hunting by introduced cats, and trapping for the pet trade.

The feet have sharp claws that help the lizard to climb trees.

This lizard of Australia has a large frill around its neck that it raises when threatened. The frill makes the lizard look larger, which may discourage *predators* (hunting animals) from attacking.

WHERE IN THE WORLD?

Found in southern New Guinea and northern Australia, ranging from Western Australia across the Northern Territory and Queensland.

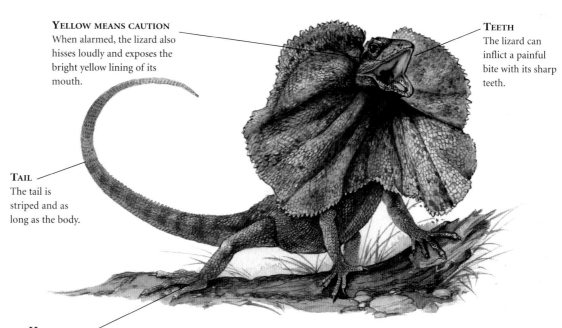

YELLOW MEANS CAUTION
When alarmed, the lizard also hisses loudly and exposes the bright yellow lining of its mouth.

TEETH
The lizard can inflict a painful bite with its sharp teeth.

TAIL
The tail is striped and as long as the body.

HIND LEGS
These are longer than the front legs, helping the lizard to run upright.

HOW BIG IS IT?

STANDING TALL
The lizard tries to scare away attackers by standing with its frill raised and its mouth opened wide. If this fails, it can also make a quick escape by running upright on its hind legs.

Strawberry Poison Dart Frog

SPECIES • *Oophaga pumilio*

VITAL STATISTICS

Length	0.65–0.95 in (1.7–2.4 cm)
Sexual Maturity	9 months
Hatching Period	Tadpoles hatch after 5–15 days; *metamorphosis* (change to adult form) takes 6–8 weeks
Number of Eggs	3–17, laid in moist leaf litter; the female carries tadpoles to pools of water
Habitat	Tropical rain forest
Diet	Ants and mites
Lifespan	3–5 years

The bright coloration of the strawberry poison dart frog warns other animals that the frog is poisonous. The skin of an adult frog can hold enough poison to kill 20,000 mice.

WHERE IN THE WORLD?

Found in Central America, in parts of Nicaragua, Panama, and Costa Rica.

ANIMAL FACTS

Native peoples use these frogs to poison blowgun darts. They use the darts to hunt monkeys and other forest animals, which tumble to the ground soon after they are hit. The frog does not rely on *camouflage* (disguise) to hide from *predators* (hunting animals). Instead, its bright colors serve as warning. However, at least one snake is immune to the frog's poison.

EYES
The eyes are relatively large, helping the frog to see well in the shadowy forest.

POISON
Many *species* (kinds) of poison dart frog have skin *glands* (organs) that produce poisonous secretions. But the strawberry poison dart frog gets its venom from the ants and other insects it eats.

FEET
The swollen toe pads at the end of the feet help the frog to climb.

Close-up of the underside of the foot

HOW BIG IS IT?

ONLY CHILD
The female carries each newly hatched tadpole to a cup at the center of a bromeliad. This plant grows up among the treetops. Each tadpole is raised separately.

African Jewelfish

VITAL STATISTICS

WEIGHT	0.3 oz (10 g)
LENGTH	Up to 6 in (15 cm)
SEXUAL MATURITY	4–6 months
NUMBER OF EGGS	200–500, laid in lines by the female and then fertilized by the male
HATCHING PERIOD	At 77 °F (25 °C), the fry emerge after 2–3 days
DIET	Feeds on insects, shrimplike animals, and aquatic vegetation
LIFESPAN	2–3 years

The African jewelfish is a cichlid *(SIHK lihd)*, a type of freshwater fish. Scientists have identified more than 1,300 *species* (kinds) of cichlids. Each is *adapted* (suited) to its own environment and type of food.

WHERE IN THE WORLD?

Found in creeks, streams, rivers, and lakes in West Africa, from southern Guinea to Liberia. Small numbers found in northern Africa, including the Nile.

ANIMAL FACTS

Cichlids are such a diverse group partly because of their unusual jaws. The fish have teeth in their throat, which frees the mouth to adapt to different kinds of foods. In a single lake, dozens of closely related cichlid species may feed on everything from *algae* (simple organisms) to insects to shrimp to fish. They may live at different depths or in particular parts of the lake. Unlike most fish, many cichlid species take care of their offspring. The male typically guards the eggs while the female digs pits in nearby sand. After the *fry* (young) hatch, the female guides them into one of the pits and guards them. She repeatedly moves the young to other pits, helping to hide them from *predators* (hunting animals). The young stay with their mother for up to a month.

PATTERNING
There are three black spots on each side of the fish's body; the gill spot is the most noticeable.

DORSAL FIN
This runs down the center of most of the back.

KILLER FISH
Some cichlids have become ambush hunters that attack and feed on other fish.

COLORATION
The female turns bright red when she is ready to breed.

PELVIC FIN
This is rounded and covered in small spots.

HOW BIG IS IT?

ADAPTABILITY

Cichlids reach their greatest diversity in the great lakes of East Africa. The mouths of cichlid species are adapted to different foods. The top cichlid eats small fish. The middle cichlid feeds on algae. The bottom cichlid sucks in tiny water animals.

Green Jay

VITAL STATISTICS

WEIGHT	2–4 oz (65–110 g)
LENGTH	9–11 in (38 cm)
WINGSPAN	About 15 in (45–55 cm)
NUMBER OF EGGS	3 eggs
INCUBATION PERIOD	18–24 days
NUMBER OF BROODS	1 a year
TYPICAL DIET	Insects and other small animals; also acorns and seeds
LIFESPAN	Unknown

Despite its striking colors, the green jay is difficult to spot among the treetops. Its green and yellow feathers help it to blend in among the leaves and its blue head looks like a patch of sky.

WHERE IN THE WORLD?

Found in South America, in Colombia, Venezuela, Ecuador, Peru, and Bolivia.

ANIMAL FACTS

Green jays are perching birds, like most other birds of the tropics. They move along the ground in small hops as they feed on insects. Green jays also have been observed using sticks to dig insects out of tree bark. The birds are graceful flying among the treetops. They are known for their many different calls and songs. One call sounds like an alarm bell. The birds build a nest in a tree or a thorny bush. The young may stay with their parents for some time, helping to raise the next group of young.

CREST
The male uses its crest of large blue feathers during courtship to attract a female.

WINGS
The short, wide wings enable the bird to fly gracefully among the tree branches.

COLORATION
The bird is yellow on its underside and green along its back. The green makes the bird difficult to spot from above the treetops, which helps to protect it from birds of prey.

HOW BIG IS IT?

SMOKE BATH
Unlike most animals, the green jay does not flee from forest fires. Instead, it often "bathes" in the smoke from smoldering trees. This unusual behavior is believed to rid the feathers of pests.

Raggiana Bird-of-Paradise

VITAL STATISTICS

WEIGHT	8.5–11 oz (240–295 g)
LENGTH	13 in (34 cm)
SEXUAL MATURITY	Males take about 5 years to grow adult feathers
NUMBER OF EGGS	1–2, pale buff with darker markings
INCUBATION PERIOD	18–20 days; young fledge by 17 days and are fed by the hen for up to 2 months
DIET	Eats mainly fruit; also some insects
LIFESPAN	Up to 33 years

ANIMAL FACTS

The appearance and behavior of the Raggiana bird-of-paradise varies by sex. Females are dull and look rather ordinary. Only the males are brightly colored, with long plumes. During the breeding season, males gather in display areas called *leks*. The lek usually has a stand of tall, slender trees. The males compete for perches on these trees. Then, they perform their displays, hoping to attract females that visit the lek. After the birds mate, the female builds a bowl-shaped nest in the fork of a tree. She cares for the eggs and young on her own. By eating fruit, these birds help to spread the seeds of many trees, including mahogany and nutmeg. Native peoples have collected the male's plumes for use in ceremonial headdresses, but this does not harm the bird.

The Raggiana bird-of-paradise is the national bird of Papua New Guinea, and it appears on the country's flag. Only males are brightly colored, with ornate plumes to impress females.

WHERE IN THE WORLD?

Found in southern and eastern parts of Papua New Guinea.

METALLIC SHEEN
The green feathers under the throat have a metallic sheen in the light.

NECK BAND
Most Raggiana birds-of-paradise have a yellow band of feathers around the neck.

LEGS AND FEET
These maintain a strong grasp on a perch even as the male bows and displays his feathers to females.

PLUMES AND WIRES
Males have reddish plumes that grow from their flanks. Wirelike feathers grow from the tail.

SHAKE YOUR TAIL FEATHERS

Males strike poses to attract females. When a female approaches the male's perch, he bows and makes noisy calls. He may clap his wings and shake his head. He can also fling his red plumes over his shoulders to expose the wires that grow from his tail. If his elaborate display impresses a female, she will join him to mate.

HOW BIG IS IT?

Termite

Termites live in large *colonies* (groups) that can have several million individuals. Although termites are sometimes called white ants, they are only distantly related to true ants.

VITAL STATISTICS

LENGTH	0.15–0.78 in (0.4–2 cm)
NUMBER OF EGGS	Queens may lay 2,000 eggs daily
DEVELOPMENT	Larvae *molt* (shed their outer skeleton) five times before they transform into adults
DIET	Wood and other plant matter
LIFESPAN	Queens 10–25 years; other termites up to a few months

WHERE IN THE WORLD?

Found in the tropics and milder areas around the world.

ANIMAL FACTS

There are thousands of *species* (kinds) of termites around the world. The termite colony forms a large family. Different members of the colony have different roles. Workers clean, maintain, and repair the nest; gather food and water; care for the young; and construct new tunnels and chambers. Soldiers defend the nest. The king and queen produce a steady supply of workers. By breaking down decaying wood and dead plant matter, termites help to maintain the balance of nature. But termites also feed on the wood people use in buildings. In fact, in locations where termites are common, people may use other building materials such as steel. Termites can also damage such crops as potatoes and sugar cane.

WORKERS
The workers perform a variety of tasks for the colony and are relatively small in size.

ABDOMEN
The *queen's* (female egg-layer's) enormous white abdomen is like an assembly line for making eggs. The rest of her body is small by comparison.

QUEEN AND KING
The queen and king are usually the only termites in the colony that breed. The king is significantly smaller than the queen.

SOLDIERS
The fearsome mouthparts and large heads of the soldiers enable them to defend the colony.

HOW BIG IS IT?

AIR CONDITIONING

Many termites build large mounds to house the colony. The structure of the mound draws in air to cool the colony. Without this cooling air flow, the sun would bake the mound and kill the termites inside.

Morpho Butterfly

GENUS • *Morpho*

VITAL STATISTICS

LENGTH	Wingspan 3–8 in (7.5–20 cm), depending on species
SEXUAL MATURITY	After leaving the cocoon
EGGS	Pale green in color
DEVELOPMENTAL PERIOD	About 20 weeks from egg to adult
HABITAT	Tropical forests
DIET	Caterpillars eat the leaves of plants; adults feed on nectar, fruit juice, and sap
LIFESPAN	Butterflies live for 4 weeks

ANIMAL FACTS

There are dozens of *species* (kinds) of morpho butterflies. But only the male morpho has wings with a metallic sheen. The metallic sheen makes males more visible to both females and other males. Males will defend their *territory* (personal area) from rivals. The metallic sheen comes from an effect known as *iridescence*. The color of most animals comes from pigment. Pigment is essentially dye, and it looks the same from any viewing angle. But iridescence is caused by the structure of the scales on the butterfly's wings. These scales break up the light, creating color indirectly. As a result, the color of the wings may appear to change as the wings are viewed from different angles.

The wings of morpho butterflies display metallic shades of blue or green. Their color does not come from pigment. Instead, it is caused by the arrangement of tiny scales, which break up the light.

WHERE IN THE WORLD?

Ranges from Mexico through Central America to South America, down to Brazil.

BODY
This is dark in color and does not have a metallic sheen.

SCALES
The wings are covered by tiny scales that have a diamond-like arrangement.

PATTERNING
Markings around the edges of the wings vary by species.

SHINY SURFACE
The metallic sheen of the wings makes these butterflies highly visible in the rain forest.

CAMOUFLAGE
The brown coloration and patterning on the closed wings allows morpho butterflies to blend into the background.

HOW BIG IS IT?

Glossary

adaptation a characteristic of a living thing that makes it better able to survive and reproduce in its environment

algae a group of simple organisms that can make their own food; some live in oceans, lakes, rivers, and streams while others live on land or in the fur of animals

amphibian one of a group of cold-blooded animals with a backbone and moist, smooth skin; many amphibians are born in the water and later live on land

antivenin a substance that counteracts a *venin* (a poisonous protein in snake and other venom)

burrow a hole in the ground that an animal uses as a home or hiding place

camouflage protective coloration that makes an animal difficult for a predator to see

canine teeth teeth present in both human beings and in other animals, used to bite or tear off pieces of food

crocodilians a group of reptiles that includes alligators, caimans, crocodiles, and gavials

domesticate to change an animal or plant from a wild to a tame state suitable for agriculture

endangered a term used by conservationists to indicate that a species is in serious danger of dying out

fish a *vertebrate* (animal with a backbone) that lives in water and has gills

footpads thick, smooth pads on the bottoms of the feet of many animals; footpads allow animals to walk quietly and they absorb some of the shock when animals jump from place to place

forage to hunt or search for food

gland an organ that makes a particular substance that the body needs

grooming a behavior in which animals clean the fur or skin of other members of their group, often of parasites

habitat the kind of place in which an animal lives

incisor a tooth having a sharp edge for cutting

insect a small, six-legged animal that as an adult has a body divided into three main parts—head, thorax, and abdomen—and a tough shell-like outer covering. Most insects also have wings and a pair of *antennae* (feelers).

mammal an animal that feeds its young on the mother's milk

marsupial a type of mammal that gives birth to tiny young that finish growing in the mother's pouch

membrane a thin sheet or layer of skin or tissue that lines, covers, or connects some part of the body

metamorphosis a series of stages in the development of some animals from their immature form to adulthood

microbe a tiny living organism; also called a bacterium or germ

molting the process of shedding feathers, skin, hair, shell, antlers, or other growths before a new growth

New World another term for the Western Hemisphere, which includes the continents of North America and South America

pack a number of animals of the same kind hunting or living together

predator an animal that preys upon other animals

primates the group of mammals that includes apes, lemurs, monkeys, and human beings

queen the egg-laying female in a colony of ants, bees, termites, or wasps

reptile an animal that has dry, scaly skin and breathes with lungs

roost the perch upon which bats, birds, and other animals rest or sleep

serrated notched like the edge of a saw

species a kind of living thing; members of a species share many characteristics and are able to interbreed

subspecies groups within a species that differ considerably from other groups in the same species

terrain an area of land having certain natural features

territory an area within definite boundaries, such as a nesting ground, in which an animal lives and from which it keeps out others of its kind

threatened a term used by conservationists to indicate that a species is in danger of dying out; threatened species are further classified as "least concern," "near threatened," "vulnerable," "endangered," and "critically endangered"

venom a poisonous substance produced by many kinds of animals to injure, kill, or digest prey

vulnerable a term used by conservationists to indicate that a species is in danger of dying out; conservationists classify animals according to their degree of risk, from "least concern" to "near threatened," "vulnerable," "endangered," or "critically endangered"

wallow to roll about in water or mud, as pigs do

Resources

Books

Breakfast in the Rainforest: A Visit with Mountain Gorillas
by Richard Sobol (Candlewick Press, 2008)
Follow a wildlife photographer into the world of the African mountain gorilla.

Rainforests by Andrew Langley (Kingfisher, 2010)
This book is a guide to the types of rain forests around the world and the animals who live in them.

Rainforest Food Chains by Molly Aloian and Bobbie Kalman (Crabtree Publishing Co., 2007)
Explore how the plants and animals of the tropical rain forests form each level of a vast food chain.

Websites

Rainforests: Exotic, Diverse, and Highly Threatened
http://www.nature.org/ourinitiatives/urgentissues/rainforests/
Learn about the wonders of the tropical rain forests—and the threats they now face—at this site from the Nature Conservancy.

Rainforest Foundation: Kid's Corner
http://www.rainforestfoundationuk.org/Kids
"Walk" rain forest trails at this educational website from the Rainforest Foundation.

Rain Forest: Incubators of Life
http://environment.nationalgeographic.com/environment/habitats/rainforest-profile/
Visitors to this website can explore photos, videos, and fun facts about the world's rain forests.

Acknowledgments

Cover photograph: Alamy (blickwinkel)

Illustrations: © Art-Tech

Photographs:

Dreamstime: 7 (K. Niecieki), 27 (H. Karius), 35 (B. Harink), 36 (C. Testi), 42 (Mesquite53), 45 (D. Hewitt)

FLPA: 6 (J. & C. Sohns), 15 (M. & P. Fogden), 16 (H. Lansdown), 17 (M. & P. Fogden), 19 (M. & P. Fogden), 20 (S.D.K. Maslowski), 29 (G. Ellis), 37 (M. & P. Fogden), 39 (M. & P. Fogden), 40 (M.B. Withers), 43 (J. & C. Sohns)

iStock Photo: 33 (R. van der Beek), 41 (S. Yagci)

David M. Jensen: 26

Photos.com: 10, 11, 12, 13, 18, 28, 30, 32, 44

Photoshots: 34 (NHPA)

Dario Sanches: 23

Stock.Xchng: 21 (A. Biggs), 38 (N. Hinks)

SuperStock: 9 (NHPA)

Eti Swinford: 14

Thinkstock: 31 (Zoonar)

Webshots: 8 (MD/72), 22 (Florence 67), 24 (Jacob 79), 25 (Urban MD Cowboy)

Index